## SUPERBASE 26

# HICKAM

# SUPERBASE 26

# HICKAM

## Hawaiian Guardians

## George Hall

**Front cover** Tanks topped off and refuelling completed, the pilot eases back behind the tanker, closes over the refuelling receptacle on the shoulder of his F-15A, and dives down below the cruising KC-135. One of 26 Eagles on strength with the 199th Fighter Interceptor Squadron (FIS), this pristine F-15A still wears full-colour Hawaiian Air Guard markings

Published in 1992 by Osprey Publishing Limited
59 Grosvenor Street, London W1X 9DA

© George Hall

ISBN 1 85532 200 5

Written and edited by Tony Holmes
Page design by Paul Kime
Printed in Hong Kong

**Back cover** The ramp level temperature at Hickam is excessive, even without the combined jet efflux of a handful of fast jets. Therefore, in an effort to keep the cockpit fittings from melting, the pilot of this Arizona Air Guard A-7D has elected to keep his canopy cranked open until he lines up at the beginning of the runway

**Title page** Holding in the standard pre-refuelling position, Vought A-7K Corsair II 80-289 tracks along at about 450 knots, high over the blue waters of the Pacific. Soon, the pilot will bank slightly to port and align himself with the flying boom, lowered into position behind the KC-135E Stratotanker. Both aircraft belong to units within the Arizona Air National Guard, the twin-stick Corsair II hailing from the 195th Tactical Fighter Training Squadron (TFTS) at Tucson International Airport, and the tanker from the 197th Air Refueling Squadron (ARS), based at the romantically named Sky Harbor International Airport in Phoenix

**Right** Hickam is not the place to practise undershooting on approach, unless perhaps you are piloting a Grumman HU-16 Albatross! An engine flame-out after take-off could also prove interesting as across the bay from the end of the runway is downtown suburbia. Let's hope the KC-135 pilot throttles up before the photo-ship joins him for a duet on the 'piano keys'

For a catalogue of all books published by Osprey Aerospace please write to:

**The Marketing Department, Octopus Illustrated Books, 1st Floor, Michelin House, 81 Fulham Road, London SW3 6RB**

# Introduction

The American military presence in the Hawaiian Islands dates back past the turn of the century. The Pacific naval units operated out of Pearl Harbor, and the Army Air Corps began developing a huge facility at nearby Hickam Field in the mid-1930s. The base was named for Lt Col Horace Meek Hickam, a famous Army aviator who was killed in a peacetime accident in 1934. By early December 1941, the Hawaiian Air Command had over 200 combat aircraft assigned to Hickam, and to the smaller Wheeler Field in the centre of the island of Oahu. Both bases were prime targets for Imperial Japanese Naval Aviation forces on the morning of Sunday, December 7th.

Hickam Air Force Base is the only American base also designated as a National Historic landmark. The old Hale Makai enlisted barracks, now the headquarters building for the Pacific Air Forces (PACAF), was heavily damaged by Japanese bombing and strafing attacks, and it still shows the chilling evidence of hundreds of hits. Wise officials resisted the temptation to restore the building to its pre-war condition, and it remains the only American air base to give continuing testimony to an unfortunate fact: every now and then, historically speaking, the bad guys roll in from nowhere with guns blazing. It happened before, and it could happen again.

Hickam today is primarily a transient base, buzzing day and night with military aircraft moving back and forth between the American mainland and the Far East. SUPERBASE HICKAM gives you a close-up look at typical activity on the tarmac: huge MAC C-141 and C-5 heavies in from Japan; a four-ship of F-111s and a pair of B-52s on their way to Australia for exercises; A-10 Warthogs in long, slow transit to Korea; a gleaming White House 707-320 making a stopover with the Secretary of State on board; a solemn ceremony beneath the rear clamshell doors of a StarLifter as the remains of Vietnam MIA's finally return to America.

The undisputed aces of the base are the 'HANGmen', the Hawaii Air National Guard and their F-15 Eagle interceptors. HANG jets stand 24-hour alert at Hickam to provide air defence for the Islands, and a huge chunk of the central Pacific. They are the only full-time Air Force tactical aircraft to be found in the Hawaiian Islands. The Marine Corps flies a bevy of F/A-18 Hornets out of MCAS Kaneohe Bay on the north side of the island; read all about them in SUPERBASE 16 KANEOHE BAY. We will also take a run up-island to Wheeler Field, now an expeditionary base for Army aviation and a déjà-vu experience for any vets of the Central Highlands campaign in Vietnam. A few miles to the west of the Hickam boundary, just beyond the ship channel leading in to Pearl, is NAS Barbers Point, a sleepy naval field hosting P-3 sub-hunters, the spooky E-6 TACAMO birds that communicate with submerged submarines, and some old but still feisty adversary A-4 Skyhawks.

Unlike any active Air Force base I've ever visited, Hickam shares its runways with the principal commercial airport in Hawaii—Honolulu International. Gaze out west from the artificial reef runway and you'll see a strange mix in the landing line-up; 747s inbound from the mainland and Japan, smaller BAe-146s that serve the other islands, and all the military cold steel you can think of. I recently taxied out in a 747 heading home to San Francisco, in a conga line made up of a KC-135 tanker, a pair of missile-laden F-15s, some A-7 Corsairs from who knows where, and a spotless white NASA C-141 bearing some sort of exotic space telescope. Hickam is a plane-gazer's dream!

Let's get out on the field, braving the always-perfect sub-tropical weather in paradise, and see what's going on. Thanks are due to Col Charlie Tucker, PACAF's head of public affairs, and SSgt Dan 'The Man' D'Antonio (an old friend from the halcyon days of the SR-71 at Beale AFB) for their terrific co-operation with this project.

# Contents

Located not too far away from Hickam is the US Navy's prime naval aviation facility, NAS Barbers Point. Home to a handful of frontline anti-submarine warfare (ASW) squadrons, the base also hosts a motley fleet of single and two-seat Skyhawks assigned to Composite Squadron (VC) One. Known locally as either the 'Blue Alii' or the 'Unique Antiquers', VC-1 perform threat simulation training for visiting naval squadrons sailing in the area aboard carriers of the 3rd and 7th Fleets, as well as regularly 'kicking Marine ass' in the shape of the three F/A-18C Hornet units which form part of Marine Air Group 24, based at MCAS Kaneohe Bay. Target towing is also a regular feature of VC-1's daily routine. Aside from its fleet of ageing 'Hot Rods', the unit also operates several large CH-53E Super Stallions as Carrier On Board Delivery (COD) aircraft

# HANGmen

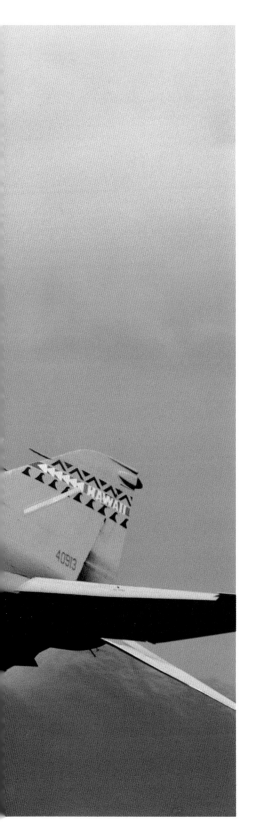

**Left** As much a part of the Hawaiian Islands as the traditional grass skirt and detectives called 'Dano', the 199th FIS has called Hickam home for 45 years. Over the decades the unit has flown the best of American 'heavy metal' from the P-47 Thunderbolt to the F-102 Delta Dagger, but perhaps its most favoured mount of all was the throaty 'Rhino', McDonnell Douglas' classic F-4 Phantom II. Receiving its first jets from the California-based 27th Tactical Fighter Wing (TFW) in October 1975, the 199th declared itself operationally ready with a change in designation from a Fighter Interceptor Squadron to a Tactical Fighter Squadron on 10 June 1976. This dramatic photograph captures F-4C 64-0913, nicknamed 'Ewa Ewa', seconds after launch as the pilot cycles away the gear. The youngest Phantom II in the 26-strong 199th TFS fleet, this particular airframe was in fact one of the very last 'Charlie' models built by McDonnell Douglas. The aircraft ended its days at Kadena AFB, Okinawa, resprayed to represent an 18th TFW F-4C of the Vietnam War period. Like many of its old squadron mates, '0913 had served with the Kadena wing during the conflict, eventually heading east to Hawaii when the 18th TFW picked up its first F-15As in 1979

**Below** Nozzles fully open and J79s screeching on zone five afterburner, 63-7632 'Ae 'o' unsticks from the Hickam black top and heads for the murky overcast. Carrying a dummy AIM-9L acquisition round on the port wing pylon, this grey veteran is heading out to the west of the islands to practise ground controlled intercepts (GCI) with a pair of 'hostile' F-4Cs which had departed Hickam an hour before

Perhaps the most significant sortie flown by the 199th in the course of a year's operations is the 'missing man' formation flight over the USS *Arizona* memorial. At 0813 hours on 7 December every year, the three-ship cruises over Pearl Harbor, commemorating to the minute Japan's assault on the US Navy base in 1941. Commencing their run in over the memorial, the four-ship soon becomes a three-ship as the pilot in the Dash-3 position opens the throttles and pulls up into the vertical, leaving his squadron mates to complete the solemn fly-by. This photograph commemorates the 1986 event, with 63-7676 'Noio' functioning as the 'missing man' on this occasion

**Above** Japan's influence on the Hawaiian islands has always been a very strong one, even before the notorious Pearl Harbor attack. Many Japanese nationals have moved across the Pacific and settled in the islands over the past 150 years, some of their descendants now flying fast jets with the 'HANGmen'. On 7 December 1985, the 199th thought it appropriate to add a little Nipponese flavour to proceedings by putting up four Phantom IIs crewed entirely by Japanese members of the squadron. Unfortunately the Navy's response to this stunt was never recorded . . .

**Left** Although the Hawaiians flew old aircraft, they armed them with the very latest versions of the USAF's staple missiles, the AIM-7L Sparrow and AIM-9L Sidewinder. Soon to take its place in the alert barn at Hickam, this European One-camouflaged F-4C sits patiently on the ramp as the groundcrew commence unshackling the rounds from the delivery trolley. All eight missiles will eventually be fitted to the Phantom II; four AIM-9s on the wing launchers and four AIM-7s recessed in the belly mountings. The missiles are all live rounds, and once the aircraft is fully armed it will be taxied over to the alert station to relieve another Phantom II

**Right** At first glance this Phantom II looks like any other F-4 operated by the 199th. However, a close examination of the paint scheme and an even closer look at the radome bullet reveals that this aircraft actually hails from the 170th TFS, Illinois ANG, and is in fact a D-model. Rapidly closing on a KC-135E of the 108th Air Refueling Squadron (also of the Illinois ANG), this Phantom II was part of a squadron det sent from the Midwest to Hawaii in December 1988 for the annual *Sentry* exercise in the Pacific. The boys from Illinois preferred the gloss grey, and subtle anti-glare panel, to the more weather-beaten matt scheme of their brothers in the 199th. The tip of the bullet fairing contains the small radar warning receiver (RWR) blisters retrofitted to the Delta model, but conspicuous by their absence on the older Charlies

**Below** This exercise also served as an operational baptism for the 'new' 199th Fighter Interceptor Squadron, the change of designation taking place when the first F-15As arrived from various units based in mainland USA and Alaska. Although the 108th ARS still trucks out of O'Hare International Airport in its Stratotankers, the 170th TFS has drastically upgraded its operational capabilities, receiving 21 slightly used F-16As and three F-16Bs from the 388th TFW at Hill AFB in Utah. The latter outfit picked up factory-fresh Charlie models as replacements. The last of the F-4Ds left Capitol Airport in Springfield in mid-1990, bound for the Davis-Monthan boneyard

**Above** Fully kitted out in his 'grow bag', G-suit and survival vest, the lean figure of four-star General Merrill 'Tony' McPeak strikes a typical fighter pilot's pose in front of a HANG F-15. Commander-in-Chief of the Pacific Air Forces (PACAF), McPeak usually flies the unit's Eagles twice a week, thus earning for himself the distinction of being the only Air Force four-star who regularly pilots a single-seat fighter. The 'Guard 'jocks' report that they would let him win if they had to, but usually they don't

**Right** Since 1957, the 199th has been charged with full responsibility by PACAF for air defence of the Hawaiian islands. In those days the unit fulfilled its mission with a mix of fair-weather F-86Es and all-weather F-86Ls. Today, the 'Guard goes about its business in the combat proven F-15 Eagle, four aircraft fully armed up maintaining 24-hour alert status all year round. Once airborne, the Eagle drivers would rely heavily on two GCI sites in the islands, manned by the 201st Combat Communications Group. This unit is vital to the 199th chances of an effective interception as there is no permanent AWACS presence at Hickam

**Below** Although most of the unit's aircraft wear the full-colour 'lei' style fin stripe that adorned their F-4s throughout the 1980s, several Eagles have begun to exhibit the worrying low-viz trend that has afflicted the Navy so dramatically over the past decade. As can be seen in this photo, the shades of grey used are noticeably darker than those present on the older semi-gloss finished F-15s

**Right** Sat comfortably on his McDonnell Douglas ACES II zero-zero ejection seat, ANG pilot Brian 'Mongo' Sakai gives his crew chief the traditional Hawaiian salute, often used between 199th squadron mates in lieu of the official version. This ancient Hawaiian symbol roughly translates to 'No Ka Oi' or 'looking good'. The low-viz 'name tag' box for the crew chief below the cockpit compares rather unfavourably with the full-colour version, which adorns many of the unit's Eagles. As with most other frontline F-15 operators, the 199th have 'Eagle Eye' sniper-scopes fitted alongside the McDonnell Electronics AN/ALQ-20 head-up display (HUD). The scope allows the pilot to identify his target once it has closed to within visual range

RESCUE

EMERGENCY ENTRANCE
CONTROL ON OTHER
SIDE

**Above** The main gear legs have just started to toe inwards as the pilot selects undercarriage retraction soon after rotation. Configured in classical 'Eagle hassling' mode, this aircraft carries a single inert AIM-9L acquisition round on the starboard launcher rail, and the almost mandatory 600-US gal drop tank on the centreline. Shimmering through the heat haze of the Eagle's twin Pratt & Whitney F100-PW-100 turbofans (here on full afterburner) are a Delta Airlines L-1011 TriStar, United Airlines 747-200, and an anonymous DC-8, all ranged up in front of the Honolulu International Airport passenger terminal

**Left** With this much action taking place on one mission, Hickam's runway could be mistaken for the Nellis black top at the height of a Red Flag exercise. Trailing the four Eagles on departure from the base are a trio of Arizona ANG F-16A Fighting Falcons, deployed to Hawaii for exercise *Sentry Tigre* 1990

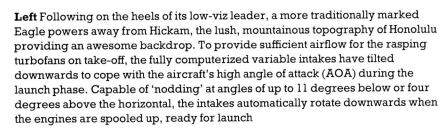

**Left** Following on the heels of its low-viz leader, a more traditionally marked Eagle powers away from Hickam, the lush, mountainous topography of Honolulu providing an awesome backdrop. To provide sufficient airflow for the rasping turbofans on take-off, the fully computerized variable intakes have tilted downwards to cope with the aircraft's high angle of attack (AOA) during the launch phase. Capable of 'nodding' at angles of up to 11 degrees below or four degrees above the horizontal, the intakes automatically rotate downwards when the engines are spooled up, ready for launch

**Below** Emulating their frontline counterparts, a pair of Eagle drivers perform a textbook two-ship departure without the use of afterburner. As the tail codes denote, these particular aircraft are amongst the oldest Eagles in service today, only the airframes based at NAS New Orleans (Alvin Callender Field) with the 122nd FIS, Louisiana Air Guard, being older. Initially issued to units in the mid-1970s, the majority of the Eagles at Hickam finished their frontline USAF service with either the 21st TFW at Elmendorf, Alaska, or the 33rd TFW at Eglin in Florida. This photograph perfectly illustrates the marked difference between the old full-colour scheme and the much more recent low-viz effort

**Above** Heading for downtown Waikiki and Honolulu, a pair of F-15s depart Runway 8 Left on military power. The stomach-churning grumble of a fast jet on launch or recovery does not seem to bother the average Hawaiian. One wonders how the locals would react if the 199th took up residence at Heathrow Airport or JFK?

**Left** Burners aglow, '083 keeps low on a Viking departure into the overcast. When this aircraft was constructed in St Louis, Missouri, in 1973, the afterburner nozzles were covered with augmentor sealing flaps, known as 'turkey feathers' to groundcrews, which in theory acted as streamlining devices, covering the complex network of sliding runners and push rods that operate the 'cans'. However, the flaps soon caused problems as they failed to mesh properly and were time-consuming and costly to maintain. The Air Force therefore decided to remove the flaps on their existing aircraft very early on in their service lives, and delete the plates completely from new-build Eagles on the assembly lines at McDonnell Douglas

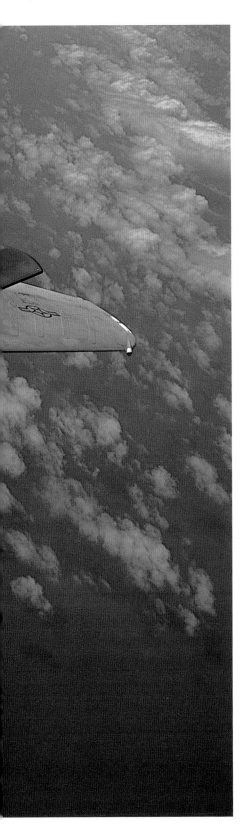

**Left** Having hassled with the visiting F-16s from the 148th Tactical Fighter Training Squadron (TFTS), Arizona Air Guard, the F-15 driver ranges up behind the Fighting Falcons' 'mothership' and prepares to top up his tanks. Crews of the 199th take full advantage of visiting KC-135s to hone their aerial refuelling techniques as, unlike many other 'Guard squadrons, they do not have a tanker unit close by to regularly work with. From this boomer's-eye view, the heavily weathered upper surfaces clearly stand out, the scuff marks over the starboard wing root being particularly noticeable. The shiny screws forming a square pattern just forward of the radome hold in place the panel which covers the Collins automatic direction-finding (ADF) sense antenna. Judging by the excessive wear around these screws, the ADF antenna features regularly on the 154th Consolidated Aircraft Maintenance Squadron's work roster

**Above** 'Mongo' Sakai holds his jet in position as the JP4 is carefully pumped from the internal tanks of the KC-135E into his F-15. The sniper scope mentioned earlier is clearly visible mounted on the instrument coaming to the left of the HUD. Reflecting in the Eagle's crystal clear canopy is the traffic light-coloured refuelling boom, painted not for the boomer's amusement but to help the receiver judge his separation distances from the tanker

**Left** As Hickam also doubles as the Honolulu International Airport, tactical breaks, and the general showmanship which tends to prevail in the skies over frontline bases, rarely takes place here. Long approaches with the gear down and landing light ablaze are the order of the day. Following his airport etiquette to the letter, a HANGman gently cruises down the glidescope towards the runway, his dorsal airbrake fully deployed in an effort to slow the Eagle up sufficiently before recovery

**Above** Mission accomplished, the Eagle driver gently flares out before kissing the tarmac with his BF Goodrich tyres. Earlier in the day, this Eagle had been one of 20 aircraft (F-15s, F-16s and A-7s) that had followed an Arizona ANG KC-135E down the runway during a SAC-style MITO (Minimum interval take-off) as part of *Sentry Tigre*

The 199th's Supervisor of Flying (SOF), Lt Col Pete Pawling mans the mike during ops out on Runway 8 Left. Comfortably ensconced within the air-conditioned confines of 'Mytai One' (the unit's ground-mobile control unit), Pawling is visually monitoring all take-offs and landings, communicating with both the tower and the Eagles through the UHF comms link mounted in the truck. He also has an FM frequency which keeps him in touch with the operations room back at the 199th's HQ. Pilots take it in turns to fulfil the SOF duty out on the runway. When not jamming on the airwaves, Pete Pawling doubles as a part-time F-15 jock, as well as being the duty pilot on the unit's sole C-130H Hercules (serial 90478)

**Above** As with aircrew the world over, the pilots of the 199th like to adorn their flying suits with appropriate unit emblems. Aside from the official Hawaiian war god (riding supersonic shock waves) patch which is worn on the right shoulder, the crews also wear this colourful little number; a miniature rendition of the official state flag. The British motif dates from the reign of King Kamehameha I, who was heavily influenced by early British explorer Captain George Vancouver around the turn of the 19th century

**Right** Commencing a twilight patrol over the islands, a singleton Eagle heads east, bathed in the warm evening light. Unlike many frontline units within today's USAF, the sun is most definitely not setting on the 199th FIS. With a full-time strength of 10Q personnel, and over 200 National Guard members spread throughout the islands, the HANGmen still have a vital role to play within PACAF

# The boys from Tucson

The Air National Guard consists of no less than 98 units operating such diverse types as the F-16A Fighting Falcon through to the HC-130H Hercules. Of these 98 squadrons, 14 of them fly this venerable warplane from bases scattered across the USA. The pugnacious A-7D Corsair II has featured prominently in ANG ranks for over 15 years, the first aircraft arriving at Kirtland AFB, New Mexico, for the 188th TFS as replacements for their weary F-100D Super Sabres in October 1975. Still flying the A-7 today, the boys from New Mexico were joined by 14 other 'Guard units as more and more Corsair IIs were freed from frontline squadrons with the advent of its replacement, the A-10 Thunderbolt II. Only one unit has since relinquished its A-7s, the 157th TFS in South Carolina becoming the first 'Guard operators of the F-16A in July 1983 when very early Block 10 Fighting Falcons were delivered to their base at McEntire, their A-7s being distributed amongst other ANG users

**Above** Sat astride his mount, the pilot waits while the final few preflight details are seen to. His 'throne' in the A-7 is a McDonnell Douglas Escapac 1-C2, this proven seat being effective at this altitude, or at ceilings as high as 50,000 feet. It can be fired whilst the aircraft is stationary, or when the pilot is trucking along at 650 knots. Activated either through pulling the primary ejection control handle 'D' between the pilot's legs, or tugging firmly down on the face curtain ejection control handle immediately above his head, the seat uses breaker prongs attached to the top of the headrest to aid the pilot's egress through the canopy. Once clear of both his aircraft and the seat, the occupant's A/P28S-20 parachute will deploy and, along with his survival kit, he will gently descend towards terra firma. The open panel just forward of the empty Sidewinder rail reveals the aircraft's LOX (liquid oxygen) bottle, and associated plumbing. A vital piece of kit which is checked and recharged after every flight, the LOX converter supplies gaseous oxygen in controlled amounts to the pilot's mask

**Left** Equipped at roughly the same time as most other Corsair II units, the 152nd TFTS said goodbye to its Super Sabres in 1977, the sleek silver century-series fighters from North America being replaced on the ramp at Tucson International Airport by 18 A-7Ds and, eventually, 15 A-7K two-seaters, all camouflaged in South-east Asian browns and greens. Fifteen years down the track, 'AZ' coded Corsair IIs still rumble around in the clear Arizona skies, although now the aircraft wear a more fashionable suit of grey, wrapped around the fuselage in two distinctive shades. Here, having seen the pilot securely strapped in and the aircraft's Allison/Rolls-Royce TF41-A-1 turbofan ignited successfully, the groundcrew tidy away the retractable loading ladder and fasten the radio and electronics bay door on the lower starboard side of the fuselage

Fuel flow checked; wing locks removed; compass set; flaps deployed; automatic flight control system (AFCS) primed; trim set; seat armed; harness secured; and canopy locked. The gloved left hand of the pilot automatically grips the chunky T-shaped throttle lever and gently pushes it forward. Whilst his hand pushes the throttle forward, his eyes are firmly glued on the cluster of dials to the right of his instrument console. The fuel flow indicator begins to wind around more rapidly; the turbine outlet temperature gauge gradually climbs, as does the oil pressure indicator, conveniently located to the right of the temperature gauge. The tachometer progressively climbs above the engine's idling speed until the pilot reaches the TF41's spool up point. His size ten flying boot then eases off the brake pedal and the Corsair II immediately springs to life, chasing its shadow down the Hickam runway. Fifty knots, sixty, seventy, the airspeed indicator reads off the aircraft's acceleration along the blacktop. The bumps and vibrations travelling through the pilot begin to flatten out as the Corsair II's momentum increases. Ninety, one-hundred knots; the pilot gently eases back on the control column with his right hand, his left staying firmly gripped to the throttle. The runway disappears under the stubby nose of the aircraft as the A-7's attitude travels through the horizontal. A quick glance to his right confirms that his station keeping with the lead A-7K is correct. As downtown Honolulu looms out of the distance, the pilot removes his left hand from the throttle and quickly reaches for the circular grip atop the landing gear control handle above the power quadrant. He pushes the lever forward and the pyramid of lights to the left of the handle stop glowing. Beneath him he feels the reassuring clunk of the twin-wheeled nose gear locking in its retracted position. As the altitude increases the pilot takes his hand off the throttle once more and reaches for the slightly curved flap control lever. Applying pressure, he extracts the handle from the flap extended gate and slides it forward to the up position, the flap attitude gauges mounted alongside the gear lights indicating clearly to the pilot that his leading and trailing edge devices have retracted. Now all he has to do is prime his radar and comms controls and he is ready for action!

The gear cycles away rapidly on the Corsair II, Vought making full use of the aircraft's tubby fuselage to house the bulky, Navy-spec undercarriage along the centreline, thus freeing the entire wing area for hardpoint fittings. The main landing gear consists of two pivoted struts (the forward one being the tension-, bending-, and torsion-resistant member, and the rear one acting as the drag brace actuator) and a single main oleo shock strut, which absorbs much of the landing forces encountered by the aircraft upon recovery. 'Guard pilots have found that when it comes to landing the A-7 its Navy lineage is best respected. No flare out is required—in fact the main gear tyres wear out quicker when the pilot chooses to flare, often resulting in the rather unpleasant scenario of a blown tyre on landing

**Above** Not all Arizona Air Guard A-7s wear the attractive grey colours, this example being one of a small minority still sprayed in the now unfashionable 1980s charcoal scheme. Being matt-based, the paint applied to the A-7s was very porous and tended to absorb moisture, thus resulting in greater corrosion problems for the groundcrews and the aircraft looking generally scruffy

**Left** Once cleaned up and cruising at altitude, the A-7 tends to look far more compact than it does on the ground. Having done his best to teach the Eagle drivers a thing or two about the tight turning circle of the A-7, the pilot cruises up behind the KC-135E and prepares to close in for refuelling. When operated by the Navy aboard its carriers, Corsair IIs, armed with a single Sidewinder on each fuselage-mounted LAU-7/A launch rail, often performed combat air patrols when a lack of suitable wind prevented F-14s from launching, or when the ship's catapults malfunctioned, the A-7 still being able to take-off from the deck without catapult assistance

Edging ever closer, the pilot of 74-1741 maintains the trail position behind the Stratotanker before getting the green light to move in. The fourth airframe built in a batch of 24 ordered in Fiscal Year 1974, this particular aircraft has spent its entire operational life in ANG hands. A total of 459 A-7Ds were built for the Air Force over a seven-year period from 1969 to 1976. The small bulge beneath the lower lip of the intake on this A-7 houses the Martin Marietta ANS-35 Pave Penny laser target detection and tracking pod. The mounting does not contain a laser itself, only a gimbal-mounted receiver which detects reflected light from a target designated by a compatible laser aimed by ground forces, or an accompanying aircraft. Information collected by the Pave Penny is fed automatically to the aircraft's Navigation/Weapon Delivery System (the heart of which is the AN/ASN-91 tactical computer), and target acquisition information is displayed on the pilot's HUD

**Above** Tanks topped up, the pilot drops behind the KC-135E, stabs in a little starboard aileron and breaks away in a gentle descending dive. The A-7's long 'sea-legs' (a result of its naval breeding) have always been appreciated by its ANG masters, the aircraft's invariably 'clean' configuration allowing squadrons to hang all manner of ordnance from its six hardpoints. The internal fuel system of the aircraft consists of six fuselage cells and an integral wing tank, giving the A-7D an operational range (in theory) of over 2300 km

**Left** The Arizona Air Guard's 33-strong Corsair II fleet is split between the operationally organized 152nd TFS, and the training optimized 195th TFTS. Both squadrons mark their aircraft with 'AZ' tailcodes and the highly stylized star and rising sun emblem synonymous with combat aircraft of this state. However, being primarily tasked with converting fast jet pilots onto the Corsair II, the latter unit tends to utilize the 15 A-7Ks far more than the singleton Deltas. Built specifically for the 'Guard' and never used by frontline USAF units, the A-7K has always suffered from paucity within its ranks — only 31 two-seaters were ever built, the last airframe leaving Vought's Dallas plant in September 1984, thus closing the Corsair II production line in the process. In this dramatic view of A-7K 80-289, the pilot's gaze is firmly planted on the tanker's traffic light display beneath the aircraft's tail, his concentration focused on keeping his mount steady as the boomer flies the refuelling probe towards the gaping receptacle grafted onto the spine of the Corsair II. Pilots have reported that when the A-7 is latched onto the 'big KC', the aircraft becomes thrust limited and has to be pulled along by the tanker, otherwise the refuelling connection separates!

Arizona is a big state, blessed with beautiful weather and relatively open skies. As a result, the Air Guard utilize these geographical and meteorological factors to their advantage, basing both the Corsair II and F-16A training squadrons within the state borders. In this photograph, elements of both the 195th and the 148th TFTSs formate in a near perfect arrow-head formation astern of the tanker. Both units share ramp space at Tucson International, thus easing the potential problems of resupplying the squadrons should they be located on opposite sides of the state. The annual two-week *Sentry Tigre* det to Hawaii has been staged by the Arizona Air Guard for several decades, strengthening the links between the two states. In fact, all Arizona Guardsmen are honorary HANGmen as well!

All alone in the Pacific skies, F-16B 79-0425 cruises along at 250 knots, way above the cool blue ocean thousands of feet below. A total of 14 two-seaters are operated by the 148th, these trainers being heavily utilized by novice 'Guard pilots newly introduced to General Dynamic's 'Electric Jet'. Like most modern 'twin stickers' developed from single-seat fast jets, the F-16B possesses identical flying characteristics to its more prolific brother, only missing out in the endurance department because of the reduced internal fuel capacity necessitated by the fitting of the extra seat in place of the forward fuselage tank. Whereas the F-16A can carry 6972 lbs of JP4 internally, the Bravo can only fit in 5775 lbs. The resulting reduction in the F-16B's operational radius is offset somewhat by its role, most training sorties tending to be much shorter in duration than specific mission taskings undertaken by frontline squadrons

The pilot has hit the switch which retracts the Universal air refuelling receptacle (UARSSI) cover, revealing the plumbing underneath. Peering up through the one-piece polycarbonate canopy, he watches the boom slowly descend from beneath the tail of the KC-135E. Once satisfied of its position, he will gently manoeuvre his lightweight fighter beneath the tanker and commence refuelling

With the two seater tanked up and clear of the boom, the singletons jockey in behind the KC-135E. Both jets appear to be identically configured, although the armourers have mounted an AIM-9L on the port wingtip of one F-16 and on the starboard rail of the other jet. In both instances, the Sidewinders are dummy rounds equipped with active seeker heads to increase the realism of the air combat manoeuvring (ACM) performed with the F-15s out over the Pacific. With the seeker fitted and fully operable, the pilot still hears the familiar growl of the missile as it tracks its target, the audible tone increasing in decibels as its tracking scan improves to lock-on and, in theory at least, 'Fox Two' launch. However, at this particular moment in the mission, the thought of a 'Fox Two' launch is probably the last thing Major Rock 'Iceman' Massey needs to be thinking about

**Above** Visitors to the Tucson home of the 148th TFTS could perhaps be forgiven for thinking that they had in fact stumbled across a long lost outpost of the Royal Netherlands Air Force (RNAF) as, aside from training potential ANG F-16 pilots, the unit also performs a similar task for ab initio 'flying Dutchmen'. Mirroring the Luftwaffe's F-4 Phantom II set up a George AFB in California, the RNAF have maintained a training syllabus in Arizona for over five years, taking full advantage of the region's excellent weather and the unit's wealth of experience on the Fighting Falcon. Of the squadron's 33 aircraft, 11 of them are actually owned by the RNAF (eight single-seaters and three twins), although these aircraft are visually indistinguishable from the rest of the 148th's fleet. Wearing a specially made patch on the sleeve of his overalls, Major Toine 'Rocky' Brekelmans prepares to don his cloth skull cap before squeezing into the HGU-55/P bonedome resting on the canopy sill

**Left** As with many Air Guard and Reserve units, the 148th TFTS operate some of the earliest F-16A/Bs built by General Dynamics. This particular airframe was part of Block 10 ordered in Fiscal Year 1979/80, which covered the purchase of 145 Alpha and 24 Bravo models

55

**Above** With not a spare seat in the house, five F-16s from the 148th TFTS screech into life as they prepare to go aloft and mix it in a running dogfight with elements of the 199th FIS. The job of these pilots is to protect the A-7s of the 152nd TFS, who have been tasked to strike an 'enemy' munitions dump somewhere north of Honolulu, as part of exercise *Sentry Tigre*

**Right** 'I wish they'd turn that racket down.' Sitting pretty on the port BF Goodrich, a 148th TFTS groundcrewman contemplates his surroundings whilst thinking about home back in Tucson. Bolted to the aircraft's centreline is a 300-US gal tank, this particular fitment being virtually standard on twin-stick F-16Bs to make up for their decreased internal fuel capacity. An extremely agile aircraft which can easily pull 9G during the course of an ACM sortie, the Fighting Falcon is only slightly restricted by external stores during a dogfight, the centre tank for example being limited to 6.5G when full and imposing no restrictions at all when empty

Whilst his passenger pushes forward to check that his straps have been tensioned properly for high-G manoeuvring, the pilot pulls out his marker pen from his shoulder holder and prepares to jot down important mission notes pertaining to course headings, radio frequencies, IFF codes and mission ceiling limitations onto his kneepad transparency. Although all of this information is logged in the aircraft's mission computer, the pilot will be able to revert to manual mode and press on with the sortie should a technical malfunction affect his electrics. A close examination of the small serial stencilled on the canopy framing immediately below the instrument coaming reveals that this particular transparency was actually fitted to the oldest F-16B in the 148th TFTS fleet in a former life, this theory being supported by the camouflage mismatch above the M61A1 cannon muzzle aperture. Now firmly affixed to airframe 79-0417, the cockpit's former home, airframe 78-0106, was built as one of 27 block 5 Fighting Falcons ordered from General Dynamics in 1979/80

**Right** Worried about flat-spotting the tyre, the 'groundie' moves aft to improve his tan with the help of the crisp exhaust gases from the F100, ticking over on idle. Actually, in reality he is in voice contact through his headset and mike with the pilot, the transmission lead being visible below the belly of the aircraft. Once he has informed the crew of his position at the rear of the jet, the pilot will wiggle his joystick and depress the rudder pedals, the all-moving tailplane and vertical surfaces on the tail twitching in response. From his vantage point at ramp level, the 'groundie' watches the moveable surfaces to ensure that all is operating as it should be. Once the all-clear call is given, the pilot will then open and close the nozzle flaps to check that the linkages between each plate are working correctly. Only after these routine (but no less vital) procedures have been carried out, will the 'groundie' whip away the wheel chocks and signal to the pilot that it is all-clear to taxy

**Above** As clean as they come, a tactical pair of F-16s depart Hickam, bound for a severe dogfighting session with the HANGmen. Taking full advantage of the aircraft's light external loadings on this occasion, both pilots begin rotation as the airspeed indicator passes through 120 knots. Blessed with an impressive thrust-to-weight ratio of better than one-to-one in clean configuration, the F-16 will unstick from the tarmac after a roll of only 1200 feet

# Visitors

'Stop the plane. I wanna catch just one more wave!' If the main drag at Heathrow or JFK looked like this I'm sure no one would bother venturing further afield than the airport perimeter track. Oh well, back to reality; this Delta Airlines L-1011 250 (an upgraded TriStar 1) is just one of 29 operated by the Atlanta based outfit. Powered by three Rolls Royce RB211-22B turbofans, the L-1011 is perfectly suited for the long over-Pacific routes serviced by Delta on the Honolulu-LAX route. The range of the big Lockheed with maximum passengers and baggage, plus sufficient international reserves of fuel in case of emergency diversion, is 2870 nautical miles. In the distance, the aircraft making a kamikaze dive at the TriStar's tail is a de Havilland DHC–7 Dash 7, a popular STOL type operated in large numbers by local airlines

Quintin V Barbieri
31 Sagamore Rd
Marblehead, MA 01945-2128

**Right** Surrounded by the standard USAF dayglo orange cones and cord (which clearly signals to all and sundry that this aircraft is not to be approached), this unique NC-135A belongs to the 4950th Test Wing, based at Wright Patterson AFB in Ohio. The only one of its type in the Air Force inventory, this aircraft has enjoyed a long and varied career since it left Boeing's Renton plant in the early 1960s. Originally constructed as a bog–standard C-135A 'troop truck' for the then Military Air Transport Command, 00371 (plus two other sister ships) was passed over to the Atomic Energy Commission and fitted out as an airborne monitoring station for use in conjunction with their above-ground nuclear tests. When the Commission 'went underground' with its test programme, the aircraft were returned to the USAF, who in turn passed 00371 onto Air Force Systems Command (AFSC). Now configured in *Project Argus* trim, the NC-135A has been heavily involved in trials connected with the Strategic Defense Initiative (SDI), more commonly referred to as 'Star Wars', across the globe. Covered in antennae and marked up as a flying 'TV test card', the aircraft is fitted with an airborne photo documentation system, which involves several optical quality windows on the port side of the fuselage; cameras equipped with high resolution film; low–light TV; an infrared spectrometer; and a sensor pointing system. The markings on the forward fuselage are used for both ground and air callibration work

**Below** Only slightly less rare than the NC-135A is this shining beauty, one of only three C-135Cs currently in USAF service, two of which are based at Hickam. Along with sister-ship 61-2671, this airframe is operated by Detachment One of the 89th Military Special Missions Wing based at Andrews AFB, Maryland. Originally delivered as C135Bs, these aircraft were modified to WC-135B specs in 1965, performing vital weather reconnaisance sorties up until 1973. 61-2668 and -2669 were then stripped of all the recce kit and reconfigured as fast staff transporters for MAC. Airframe 61-2671 was modified accordingly the following year, and along with '2668, was issued to Det 1 to haul both the CINCPAC admiral and PACAF four–star general across the vast expanses of the Pacific

There is only one pretty C-141 Starlifter in existence and this is it. Operated by NASA, the aircraft is based at their expansive Ames Research Center at NAS Moffett Field, California. However, during a typical year's flying, the C-141 spends a lot of its time operating from remote sites across the globe in an effort to obtain the best possible observing conditions for its internally mounted 36-inch infrared telescope. During a typical sortie the aircraft will climb to over 45,000 feet, above the earth's smog layer and away from light pollution, so that the astrophysicists aboard the C-141 can clearly observe the heavens. The telescope itself (a forerunner of the Shuttle-mounted Hubbell device) is operated through a sophisticated star-tracking system, which allows astronomers at their consoles to 'fly' the aircraft via a direct link flight control system once a constellation has been sighted. Seen here en route for Auckland, New Zealand, on a six month deployment, the C-141 has been christened 'Kuiper' after the distinguished American astronomer Gerald P Kuiper

Sharing ramp space with the C-141 at Hickam was Canadian Armed Forces (CAF) CC-130E 130308, the oldest Hercules in the CAF fleet. Based at Canadian Forces Base (CFB) Edmonton, the aircraft belongs to No 435 Squadron, who on this occasion had been tasked with resupplying vessels of the CAF Navy cruising near the Hawaiian Islands during exercise *RIMPAC '90*. Loaded up with vital ships' spares, mail and replacement sailors, the aircraft maintained a shuttle service between Hawaii and Canada's west coast throughout the exercise period. The CAF presently operates a mixed fleet of 28 CC-130s, comprising twenty-two E-, two H- and four N-models, equipping No 429 OCU at CFB Winnipeg, No 435 Sqn at CFB Edmonton and No 436 Sqn at CFB Ottawa

Hailing from the same Lockheed production line in Georgia as the CC-130E, this Hercules has been optimized to perform the more specialized task of air-to-air refuelling. Assigned to VMGR-352 Det C, and based at MCAS Futenma in the Okinawan Islands, this KC-130R is just one in a fleet of over 50 tankers shared between three refuelling units, one of which is reserve manned. The Hercules is a regular visitor to MCAS Kaneohe Bay, where its refuelling abilities are fully utilized by the three F/A-18C squadrons of Marine Air Group 24. Situated on the south-eastern side of Ohau, 'K-Bay' possesses only limited ramp space, so when parking becomes a problem the KC-130 will often operate from the larger Hickam pan

**Above** Being strategically sited in the middle of the world's largest ocean, Hawaii is often visited by aircraft transitting across the globe heading to or from an exercise thousands of miles from home. One such type to chock its tyres on the Hickam ramp in 1990 was this faded VC10K3 'Super' of No 101 Sqn, despatched to the Far East in support of Royal Air Force Tornado GR.1s participating in the annual *Golden Eagle* exercise. As with the other eight VC-10s in service with the squadron at RAF Brize Norton, this aircraft performed sterling work in the Persian Gulf during both *Operation Desert Shield* and *Desert Storm*

**Right** Although the ubiquitous Sea King possesses a long range, it would take a gale force tail wind and a fuel tank the size of its passenger cabin to allow this helicopter to travel a quarter of the distance between Victoria, British Columbia, and NAS Barbers Point. Therefore, the only way to cross the vast blue swells of the Pacific without having to resort to swimming the last few thousand miles is to embark aboard a Canadian Armed Forces naval vessel, and let the ship do all the hard work! Blending in well with the tropical storm clouds behind it, this CH-124 hails from the oiler HMCS *Provider,* which was moored in Pearl Harbor during a break in the exhaustive *RIMPAC '90* exercise. This particular aircraft is one of four CH-124s based on the Canadian west coast at 'Pat Bay' (Victoria International Airport). These helicopters are tasked with supporting the small naval presence on this side of Canada, the remaining 30-strong fleet of Sea Kings being based at the large CFB facility at Shearwater in Nova Scotia. These latter aircraft are shared between Nos 406, 423 and 443 Sqs

When you're trying to catch a Japan Airlines 747 it pays to use a thick line preferably connected to a Hughes 500! No, seriously, this canary yellow cab belongs to the Honolulu Fire Department, and when its not putting out small conflagrations, it's winching 'wiped-out' bathers from the wild surf that surrounds the islands. Here, the pilot brushes up on his extraction skills in a quiet corner of the Hickam Field. Although possessing only a modest lifting capability, the veteran '500 has proven ideal for emergency work because of its minimal cold start reaction time. Perhaps the Fire Departmnet should think about respraying the Hughes gloss black with orange trim and finding a large black guy with Vietnam War experience (preferably knicknamed 'TJ') to fly it, aka 'Magnum PI'

# The Army

Talking about Vietnam, the US Army facility at nearby Wheeler Army Air Field has been styled along An Khe lines, looking for all the world like a 1960s base in the Central Highlands. Part of the 1st Battalion's 25th Aviation Regiment, these AH-1Gs and UH-1Hs sit quietly in the early morning mist prior to the start of the day's flying. Only the flat plate windscreen and the M65 Laser Augmented Airborne TOW (LAAT) sighting unit in the nose give the Vietnam ruse away, the G-models of 20 years ago having curved perspex canopies and only a basic sight for the gunner sat up front. Although many AH-1Gs have been modified and upgunned with the M197 20 mm rotary cannon (redesignated AH-1Ss), the Cobras in Hawaii are still fitted with the Vietnam-era M28 turret housing either a pair of 7.62 mm machine-guns or two M129 grenade launchers, or a mixture of both. Beneath the stub wings on both Cobras are M159 19-shot 70 mm FFAR (Folding-Fin Aircraft Rocket) pods inboard, and paired M65 TOW (Tube-launched, Optically-tracked, Wire-guided) tubes for the BGM-71 anti-tank missile outboard

Accompanied by its traditional calling card, the distinctive Bell 'whock, whock', a nondescript UH-1H hover taxies across the grass, bound for the Regiment dispersal. Of all the versions of Huey built by Bell, the Hotel model has been easily the most popular, the US Army alone taking 5435. Aside from the unofficial Cougar's head on the nose of this aircraft, the Huey wears the standard US Army CARC (Chemical Agent Resistant Coating) finish overall. Virtually black in colour, the CARC paint has good radar and infrared absorbent characteristics, and is treated to allow chemical contaminants to be removed far easier and safer than from the old olive drab finish. The triangular prongs fitted above and below the cockpit are wire cutters

**Above** Aside from the Hueys at Wheeler Field, several modified UH-1V helicopters are permanently based at Hickam providing airborne medevac flights for both military and civilian casualties across Oahu. Other than these Hueys, there is no non-military helicopter 'life flight' capability in Hawaii. Approximately 220 UH-1Hs were converted by the Army's Electronic Command at Lakehurst, New Jersey, for the medevac role. The mods included the fitment of improved avionics, a glide slope indicator, ARN-124 DME (Distance Measuring Equipment) and a radio altimeter. To help in the physical retrieval of injured patients, the helicopters were also equipped with a winch, the head of which is just visible behind the pilot's shoulder

**Right** As these aircraft increase in age, so too do the maintenance problems. Recently, a number of Huey operators have experienced tail pylon fatigue in their UH-1s, forcing helicopters to be grounded whilst strengthening repairs have been carried out. This technician is checking the tension levels in the tail rotor drive gearbox, this vital piece of kit connecting the tail rotor transmission shaft with the tail rotor drive shaft

**Above** Perhaps the rarest aircraft to wear 'stars and bars' in Hawaii is this gleaming Grumman Gulfstream 1. Unique in the Army's inventory, the aircraft was confiscated from drug-runners and given to the high command at Wheeler Field for use as a senior officers' hack. Fitted out in executive fashion, the Gulfstream is very popular with ranking personnel as its twin Rolls-Royce Dart turboprops power the aircraft along at an impressive 320 knots. Couple this speed with the Gulfstream 1's long legs (2540 miles on max internal fuel), and it is easy to see why the aircraft is so desirable. Aside from this solitary airframe, two VC-4As are used in a similar VIP role by the US Coast Guard, whilst the US Navy still operates eight of the nine TC-4C Academe airframes delivered in 1968/69. These latter aircraft are heavily utilized in the training of bombadier/navigators for the A-6 Intruder community

**Left** Brightening up the landscape a little with its glossy green and white paint scheme, this Beech C-12C is one of a pair of VIP configured Super King Air 200s attached to Wheeler Army Air Field. Along with the 'comfortable' C-12s, a single RU-21D Sigint (Signals Intelligence) electronic warfare aircraft is assigned to the Hawaiian Army National Guard, this more specialized airframe also being based at Wheeler Field

# Naval aviation

The island of Oahu has long been viewed as a 'natural aircraft carrier' by the US forces, hence the high proportion of aircraft from all four branches of the service scattered across its craggy topography. Six miles west of Hickam is NAS Barbers Point, traditionally home to Patrol Wing Two (PATWING 2). Along with PATWING 10 at NAS Moffett Field, California, the Orions at Barbers Point are controlled by Commander Patrol Wings Pacific (COMPATWINGSPAC). Five squadrons equipped with predominantly C-model P-3s fly out of Barbers Point, patrolling one of the largest 'beats' assigned to any maritime patrol force in the world today

The good thing about modern Navy Orion markings is that if you want to see a machine that belongs to say VP-1 'Screaming Eagles' for example, you can easily convince yourself that this particular aircraft is the one that you are after. Similarly, this self-same Orion can belong to VP-4 'Skinny Dragons', VP-6 'Blue Sharks', VP-17 'White Lightnings' or VP-22 'Blue Geese', if you so wish. Therefore, in one go you have witnessed a P-3 from each of the units in PATWING 2! How accommodating the Navy are to our needs. One wonders, however, what a sailor from VP-4 does when he is instructed to replace a circuit breaker in squadron airframe number seven though . . .

**Above** Although operating a comparatively small fleet of Hercules when compared to the USAF, the Coast Guard nevertheless has a rich history of C-130 operations from which to draw upon. Starting with a modest dozen HC-130Bs in the late 1950s, the Coast Guard has gone on to operate HC-130E and H-models in larger numbers. Based at five USCG air stations on the American seaboard, the HC-130s usually number four or five airframes per base. This glossy HC-130 is one of three Hotel models stationed at NAS Barbers Point, which, along with a solitary HC-130E, are tasked with patrolling the central Pacific region

**Left** At the end of 1990 VPs -1, -4 and -17 operated baseline P-3Cs and VP-6 was still equipped with the decidedly passe P-3B. The odd squadron out here is VP-22, the 'Blue Geese' being the crack unit in PATWING 2 flying the Update II.5 version of the Charlie model. Therefore, by looking closely at this Orion on launch from Barbers Point, which exhibits all the tell-tale signs of an Update II.5 (underwing stores pylons and chin doors for the retractable forward-looking infrared (FLIR) turret), it would be safe to say that this particular airframe hails from VP-22. Perhaps the clincher on this is the small bulge just aft of the sonobuoy launchers, which houses an aft-facing camera for battle damage assessment. All three baseline P-3C units are scheduled to receive Update I airframes soon, whilst the 'Blue Sharks' of VP-6 should receive Update II.5s by the end of 1992

**Above** The Army may have the rarest aircraft on Oahu, and the Air Force the fastest, but the Navy easily operates the most expensive. Valued at well over $100 million a unit, the brand new Boeing E-6A Hermes TACAMO (Take Charge and Move Out) has only recently made its operational debut with VQ-3 'Ironmen', flying its first sortie on 31 October 1989. Built as a partial replacement for the venerable EC-130Q Hercules TACAMO, the E-6A will also eventually serve with VQ-4 'Shadows' at NAS Patuxent River, Maryland. Based on a nuclear-hardened version of the venerable Boeing 707-320B, 16 Hermes have been built for Navy use, their primary role being to serve as a communications link between the National Command Authority in the USA and ballistic missile submarines on patrol in the Pacific or Indian Oceans. To allow it to perform this task the E-6A is jammed full of satellite communications equipment, aerials for which can be seen on each wingtip

**Left** Powered by four CFM International F108-CF-100 turbofans, the E-6A effortlessly (and rather more quietly than a KC-135A) climbs out of Barbers Point. At the base of the tail can be seen a small fairing with a red cone protruding from it. This modification provides part of the vital link between the various command posts (ACP) and the submarines. In a typical scenario the E-6 will link 'upward' with the ACPs and the Presidential E-4, plus to satellites and to the communications systems aboard armed ICBMs. Message traffic 'downward' to the submarines will be passed via a secure very low frequency (VLF) Litton LTN-211 system. This consists of a 26,000-foot long antenna trailing wire aerial (LWTA), with a 41 kg drogue at the end, which is winched out through an opening in the cabin floor. The 4000-foot shorter trailing wire (STWA) is deployed from the tail of the aircraft, this device acting as a dipole. Once the aerials are deployed the Hermes enters a tight orbit and the drogue stalls, falling almost vertically. Below the surface a submarine will be trailing a towed buoyant wire antenna which will pick up any signals relayed from the E-6A. To help keep operating costs down, both VQs -3 and -4 could eventually be relocated to Tinker AFB, Oklahoma, where support facilities for similar E-3 Sentry aircraft are located

# SAC and MAC

Resembling a *Desert Storm* strike package en route to its target, three 148th TFTS F-16s hold perfect formation on the wingtips of a KC-135E from the 197th ARS. All hailing from Arizona, the mixed formation had met up out over the Pacific during the first refuelling stint for the fighters, bound for Hawaii. Along with the A-7Ds of the 152nd TFS, the Fighting Falcons were bound for Hickam, and exercise *Sentry Tigre,* a two-week long ANG fighter derby held annually. Total flight time for the Arizona ANG boys was six hours, cruising at about 450 knots. On a TransPac like this one, the autopilot would be chopped in early and the paperback retrieved from the map case, the pilot resuming manual control only to perform his aerial refuelling, and finally his recovery at Hickam

Closing in on Hickam's Runway 8 Left, the pilot powers in with the KC-135E's flaps fully deployed. At the end of a long flight, which has seen the aircraft controlled predominantly by autopilot, the aircrew have to be particularly vigilant to ensure that the landing is performed as a matter of routine, ending a successful, and complex, TransPac mission on the right note. The approach to Hickam's blacktop sees the aircraft overflying land which has been periodically reclaimed and built upon by both the USAF and the Honolulu International Airport Authorities. To the aircraft's left are the Zulu Alert barns for the 199th FIS's F-15As, whilst immediately ahead is the urban sprawl of downtown Honolulu

Seconds away from touchdown, the pilot gently flares the aircraft out before alighting. Now possessing eight KC-135Es and charged with fulfilling any refuelling requirements the state's three fighter squadrons may have, the 197th ARS have not always been in tankers, initially being equipped with P-51D Mustangs. The squadron's lineage stretches back to the 412th FS/373rd FG of the 9th Air Force, flying P-47 Thunderbolts in Europe from May 1944 to VE Day. Reassigned to the ANG in 1946, the unit was redesignated the 197th FS in the process, initially being based at Luke Field and then moving to its current home at Sky Harbor in 1948. The jet age embraced the 'Copperheads', as they are colloquially known in Arizona, in November 1950 when the first F-84Bs arrived in Phoenix. Soon after, the unit was called up to active duty and tasked with training Thunderjet pilots at Luke AFB for service in Korea. Returning to ANG control in late 1952, the squadron briefly flirted with P-51s once more, before receiving some well-used F-86A Sabres from a frontline unit. The Alphas were replaced by Limas in November 1957, which in turn gave way to F-104A Starfighters in April 1960. As with the F-84 a decade before, the unit's re-equipment with a new type coincided with its call up to active duty, the 197th FIS being summarily despatched to Ramstein AB in Germany as part of the ANG's commitment to the Berlin Crisis of 1961. Upon returning to Arizona in 1962, the unit's mission tasking was drastically changed and the Starfighters made way for C-97G Stratofreighters. Redesignated the 197th Air Transport Squadron, the 'Copperheads' operating the venerable Boeings until 1972 when the more specialized KC-97L tanker version replaced the bog standard freighters. Now redesignated as the 197th ARS, the unit eventually received more modern equipment in the form of the KC-135A Stratotanker in October 1977, trading up to the more powerful KC-135E some years later

Tracking along the coral-based taxyway out towards the main strip, this nondescript KC-135R belongs to the 93rd ARS, one of three units (the 924th ARS with KC-135As and the 328th BTS equipped with B-52Gs being the other two) within the 93rd Bombardment Wing at Castle AFB, California. The Romeo model Stratotanker is the 'Cadillac' of the KC-135 family, possessing buckets of power generated by its four 'fat' F108-CF-100 (CFM56) turbofans. Originally built in the early sixties as a standard Alpha model, this airframe, like many others, was upgraded with new powerplants in the mid-eighties. Aside from the prominent turbofans, the 'new' KC-135Rs were also fitted with a dual quick start auxiliary power unit ( APU) to cut down engine spool up time; a Turbine Engine Monitoring System (TEMS); Air Data Computer (ADC); improved landing gear; a Flight Control Augmentation System (FCAS); and Mk III anti-skid five-rotor disc brakes. The turbofans themselves produce roughly 24,000 lbs of thrust, compared to the thirsty early generation Pratt & Whitney J57 turbojets which pumped out 14,000 lbs max. Aside from the power benefits, the F108s are also quieter and virtually smokeless

**Left** Not all the KC-135s in service with the 197th ARS wear the drab charcoal grey that has become fashionable in Strategic Air Command (SAC) ranks of late. This airframe, serial 53143, still retains its traditional SAC grey, suitably trimmed with the unit colours on the fin and the distinctive star-spangled sash around the waist. This aircraft is in fact the most senior airframe assigned to the squadron and is the second oldest tanker in the 104-strong ANG KC-135E fleet. The re-engined Echo models are used almost exclusively by 'Guard squadrons, who traded in their well-worn KC-135As for 'turbofanned' tankers in the mid-eighties. As well as changing the J57s for TF33-P-102s, the Air Force also specified the fitment of a cartridge start capability on the aircraft. Boeing 707 horizontal stabilizers were also utilized, an improved electrical system fitted, thrust reservers installed within the engines, and a yaw damper built in. All these improvements have made the venerable Stratotanker a far more pleasant proposition to fly and maintain

**Below** Unfortunately one of the problems regularly encountered by the ANG pilots at Hickam is the traffic jam that tails back from the runways, delaying both civil and military aircraft alike. Sitting in the midday sun in a drab KC-135 is no fun at all, but spare a thought for the suited-up 'jet-jocks' esconced in their little A-7s immediately ahead of the tanker. Tightly strapped in and covered in survival equipment, these guys have to leave the canopies cranked open until the very last minute, keeping the ambient temperature within the cockpit down to just below boiling point. Ahead of them, several F-16s, a pair of 737-200s and a single L1011 wait patiently for another TriStar to land and clear the runway

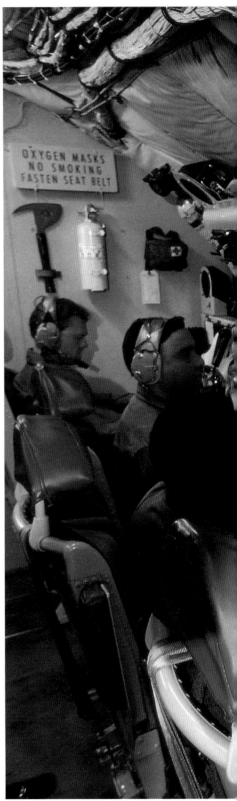

**Above** Basking under a typically azure blue Hawaiian sky, a highly modified EC-135J of the 9th Air Command and Control Squadron (ACCS) is primed for another marathon mission over the Pacific. Only four Juliet model EC-135s currently appear on the Air Force's operational listings, and they all reside at Hickam. Jam packed with communications equipment, these aircraft were originally delivered to the USAF in the 1960s as TF33-powered C-135Bs. Pulled from service almost immediately, they were suitably modified and issued as EC-135C 'Looking Glass' airframes to the 1st ACCS at Offutt AFB, Nebraska. Eventually replaced by the far larger Boeing E-4B in 1979/80, these airframes (which had been modified to J-model specs in 1965/66) were sent westward to Hickam, where they have remained ever since performing regular *Blue Eagle* missions for CINCPAC

**Right** A very large shoehorn was used when the equipment was squeezed inside the slender confines of the EC-135, as this photo clearly shows! Low frequency, high frequency, satellite and trailing antenna systems are all fitted within the airframe, associated blade aerials festooning the external surface of the aircraft. Tasked with providing Post-Attack Command and Control for the Pacific region, these EC-135s would allow the CINCPAC staff to continue controlling military operations after the first wave of enemy ICBMs had impacted their targets. These airborne command posts are also capable of maintaining a constant communications link with other similarly equipped aircraft

**Above** From this head-on angle many of the lumps and bumps associated with the EC-135J are clearly visible. The prominent black fairing midway along the fuselage contains the aerial for the high frequency communications equipment. Utilized when transmitting to ground stations, this system is believed to form part of the AN/ARC-96 high frequency/very low frequency electronics suite. The trio of white blisters flanking the aerial contain equipment associated with the aircraft's impressive satellite navigation system, which allows the crew to attain accurate global positioning without having to rely on ground stations. The crew can also communicate with orbiting satellites using this system. The various blade aerials immediately behind the cockpit are used in connection with the aircraft's wide frequency ranging transmitters and receivers

**Right** Cruising high over the tropical cloud base off the Hawaiian islands, a pristine KC-10A wearing tradtional SAC markings prepares to descend into the murk and claw its way into Hickam. Although the aircraft is blessed with full leading and trailing edge slats and flaps, only the small high-speed ailerons on both wings appear to be in use. The KC-10 well lives up to its service name of Extender, possessing a range of over 18,500 km unrefuelled. Within its huge bulk, the Extender fits seven unpressurized fuel bladder cells under the fuselage decking, leaving the aircraft's cavernous interior free to hold up to 30 standard USAF 463L pallets

Having successfully negotiated the stormy weather that often socks out Honolulu in the 'winter', a drab KC-10A from the 22nd Air Refuelling Wing (ARW) kisses the tarmac after flying in non-stop from its home at March AFB, California. The USAF could only afford 60 KC-10s, 59 of which are still in service today split between the 22nd ARW, the 4th Tactical Wing at Seymour Johnson AFB, North Carolina, and the 2nd Bombardment Wing at Barksdale AFB, Louisiana. The March wing itself is made up of the 6th and 9th Air Refuelling Squadrons, who share a pool of 20 Extenders. Other than the 22nd ARW's Army Air Corps badge on the tail, and the odd flash of individual nose art, the KC-10s are devoid of distinctive squadron markings

Of all the visiting aircraft that regularly enjoy the delights of a Hawaiian stopover at Hickam, this behemoth is without a doubt the most impressive. One of a quartet of Boeing E-4s built from the standard 747-200 airframe to USAF order in the late 1970s, this aircraft is seen disgorging some of its crew from a forward hatch, having just completed a training sortie out over the Pacific. Originally delivered as an E-4A kitted out with equipment stripped from an EC-135 and powered by JT9D engines, this airframe was brought up to Bravo standards in the early 1980s with the fitment of more advanced electronics and four General Electric F103 turbofans. These astronomically priced (US $100 million each) aircraft fulfil the National Emergency Airborne Command Post (NEACP or 'Kneecap') tasks for the US forces, operating with a crew of 94 (which can be increased by 30 battle staff) on a main deck level which has been split into six work stations. These areas are the National Command Authorities section, the briefing room, the conference room, the battle staff communications control centre and the rest area. Various frequency communications equipment is fitted within the airframe, the 'doghouse' atop the traditional 'Boeing bulge', for example, housing antennas for the super high frequency system. All four E-4Bs are based at Offutt AFB, Nebraska, as part of the 1st ACCS, which is in turn controlled by the 55th SRW

MAC provides the vital supply 'air bridge' for the USAF units stationed abroad, carrying everything from bullets and baked beans to engines and envelopes. Cargo flights from the 'States arrive and depart from Hickam on a daily basis, the drab C-141s and C-5s being ranged up on their own purpose-built ramp close to the main runway. Virtually all MAC units pass through the islands in the course of a year, these nondescript StarLifters hailing from the 443rd Military Airlift Wing (MAW) at Altus AFB, Oklahoma, and the 63rd MAW at Norton AFB, California, respectively. As with all the USAF StarLifters, these airframes have received the Lockeed stretch 'plugs', which have drastically increased the aircraft's load carrying capacity. A total of 284 C-141As were delivered to the USAF, of which 270 were later rebuilt as stretched C-141Bs. Rather surprisingly, the StarLifter's cargo hold cross-section is identical (10ft x 9ft) to the Hercules, a factor which has hindered the C-141's outsize load carrying capacity over the years

Over the years the USAF has taken great pleasure in developing roles for the ubiquitous Hercules, turning sedate, cargo-hauling C-130s into 'Spectre' gunships or 'Combat Talon' Special Forces aircraft. This particular 'Herk', seen contrailing its way down the Hickam blacktop, has survived two conversions during its service life however, neither of which have involved fitting guns in the fuselage! Assigned the specialized role of weather reconnaissance, this veteran Hercules is one of 11 WC-130s allocated to the 55th Weather Reconnaissance Squadron (WRS), based at McClellan AFB in California. Initially built as a rescue HC-130 (hence the angular radome), this airframe was completely stripped of its mission specific equipment and refurnished with metrological and electronic sensors. Whereas most pilots avoid bad weather, the aircrew assigned to the 55th WRS go in search of hurricanes, typhoons and cyclones, monitoring the conditions encountered within them for future analysis. Several specific taskings exist for WC-130 crews; *Volant Ghost* has them gathering data in spots not properly covered by sophisticated monitoring equipment, any data gleaned being passed to the USAF's Global Weather Center; *Volant Eye* involves WC-130s tracking hurricanes on both US coastlines, and in the Gulf of Mexico; whilst *Volant Cross* sees missions being generated specifically to gather relevant data in support of overseas TAC deployments. At press time, the unit was scheduled for deactivation, its aircraft being reassigned to the reserve-manned 815th Tactical Airlift Squadron at Keesler AFB, Mississippi

Lockheed's MAC heavyweights share ramp space at Hickam on a warm afternoon. Whereas most StarLifters now wear the more tactical 'lizard' colours, the odd C-141 can still be found in the traditional glossy grey and white, these airframes often performing non-standard tasks like famine relief or the emergency repatriation of American citizens from strife-torn Third World countries. It has been found in the past that the authorities in many of these politically sensitive nations are far more willing to co-operate with the crew of a USAF aircraft that looks outwardly more like a civil airliner, rather than a fully blown 'camo' Starlifter that could easily be chocked full of the 82nd Airborne!

**Above** When tasked with bringing home the remains of possible MIAs from Vietnam and Laos, the 60th MAW at Travis AFB, California, ensured that their pristine gull grey and white C-141B (64-0643) was the aircraft that performed this solemn flight. Greeted by a full guard of honour that included members from all branches of the armed forces, the aircraft was relieved of its precious cargo by hand-picked pall-bearers. Once the ceremony had finished, the remains were passed on to a special team of pathological scientists, who then conducted complex tests in Honolulu in an effort to establish their identity. A formal ceremony is always staged as a mark of respect for returning MIAs at Hickam

**Right** Throttles wide open and turbofans whining, a blotchy C-5B departs Hickam's long coral runway with plenty of room to spare. Powered by four purpose-built General Electric TF39-1C engines, the Galaxy has never suffered from a shortage of breath, even when fully loaded and operating in the tropics. The TF39-1C is the most modern version of GE's huge turbofan, the powerplant possessing a 'bump rating' capacity which allows the pilot to temporarily use 43,000 lbs of thrust from each engine during maximum-weight take-offs

The StarLifter is large, but the real 'Big MAC' is the C-5 Galaxy, the Command's favoured heavy hauler for TransPac resupply sorties. Prominent in these head-on views are the massive wing leading edge slats that have remained locked in the extended position after the aircraft has landed. These devices are crucial in the critical stages after take-off and before landing, improving the lift generated by the wing and providing the pilot with greater control over the behemoth Galaxy at lower speeds. Driven by a hydraulic motor, the four inboard slats on each wing are sealed, whilst the three outboard sections are slotted

# Hickam highlights

**Right** Unlike many US bases in mainland America, Hickam has changed very little over the past 50 years. Indeed, only the C-135C in the foreground and the odd post-war high-rise building on the far shores of Pearl Harbor date this photo at all, the airfield itself and the naval base behind looking very much like they did on 7 December 1941. Bang in the centre of this panoramic view, just to the right of the chequered water tower, is the *Arizona* memorial

**Below** Pan around 180° and the expansion of the base to accommodate the large MAC transports and more potent ANG fighters is more far evident. The transport ramp is clearly visible, as is the carefully manicured golf course—a vital facility at any PACAF base. Behind the complex criss-cross of taxyways and hardstands is the 14,000 ft reef runway, connected at either end to the base itself by coral causeways. Behind the MAC ramp in Hickam's second stretch of black top, Runway 8 Left. Immediately above the small striped military control tower near the centre of the photo are the white Zulu alert barns for the ANG F-15s

Geographically positioned in the centre of the base is the Hale Makai complex of circa 1930s offices, all well maintained and surrounded by vibrant foliage. Currently the PACAF headquarters building, these offices served as enlisted barracks in 1941, and as such were a designated target for attacking Imperial Japanese Naval aircraft on the morning of 7 December. The building was repeatedly strafed during the raid and over 40 men were killed. In the aftermath of the attack, the Army Air Force decided to leave the external battle damage intact to serve as a constant reminder to future generations of the heavy price paid by the USAAF at Hickam, Wheeler and Bellows fields

**Above** Because of its huge 14,000 ft crushed coral runway, Hickham has been assigned the role of emergency alternate landing site for the Space Shuttle should weather factors make recovery at Edwards impossible. The most visible permanent reminders of this unique tasking are the huge striped barriers at the threshold of the runway

**Left** Period hangers and lush vegetation of Honolulu make Hickam one of the more unique bases in the USAF and also one of the most popular overseas postings for service personnel

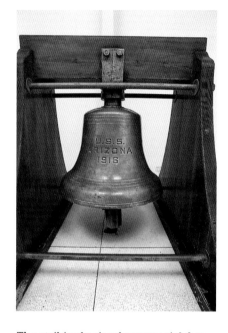

The strikingly simple memorial that has been erected over the sunken battleship USS *Arizona* is a popular spot with visiting tourists. The battleship was straddled by bombs in the tight confines of Pear Harbor, the vessel exploding and sinking rapidly after the ship's magazines were hit. Over 1300 sailors were entombed in the *Arizona*, their remains never being recovered. The memorial sits astride the submerged warship, which is plainly visible in the clear tropical waters of the harbour. Oil still bubbles from the wreck 50 years after the battleship was sunk. One small artifact that has been removed from the vessel and put on display is the ship's bell, which bears the *Arizona's* commissioning date

**Above** Both Wheeler Field and Hickam have an impressive collection of gate guards spread throughout their respective grounds. The oldest aircraft on display is this rare Curtiss P-40K, resident in Honolulu for many years. To a warbird collector back in the US this airframe, even in its battered and well-weathered state, would be worth at least $500,000. Looking remarkably intact for its advancing years, this historically significant aircraft deserves to be fully restored and permanently displayed indoors, Hangar One at Hickam being a suitable final resting place

**Left** A little younger than the P-40K, and having just benefitted from a thorough refurbishment, this elegant B-25J Mitchell looks set to weather a few more years in the tropics. Having survived the massive scrapping programme of war surplus airframes instigated by the US government immediately after VJ day, this B-25 was stripped of its .50 calibre Browning mountings and converted into a fast VIP transport for the fledgling PACAF. After many years of service the airframe was eventually retired, being presented to Hickam in due course. Funnily enough, the Hawaiian Air Guard never actually used the Mitchell, instead receiving the slightly more modern Douglas B-26C Invader to operate on long-range island patrols alongside its P-47N Thunderbolts

**Above** Several F-86 Sabres are preserved at Hickam, this particular E-model honouring the USAF's ranking ace of the Korean War, Captain Joseph D McConnell Jr. Assigned to the 25th FIS/51st FIW, McConnell achieved a score of 16 kills over North Korea, the majority of these being MiG-15s. The aircraft is beautifully restored in period colours, only a lack of gaudy fuselage art and the modern ejector seat warning triangle detracting slightly from the finished jet's superb appearance. The 199th FIS was the recipient of war-weary F-86Es in February 1954, these combat-proven jets replacing the last remaining P-47Ns in 'Guard service

**Right** Continuing on the Sabre theme, the HANGmen traded in their fair weather F-86Es for radar-equipped F-86L 'Sabredogs' in the spring of 1958, these aircraft allowing the 199th to protect the islands' sovereignty on a 24-hour basis, in any weather. The redesigned nose of the aircraft contained an APG-36 search radar, which controlled the firing of a rocket pack mounted flush in its belly. Once lock-on had been achieved on the target, the tray would lower into the slipstream and the rockets would be fired off in salvoes. Of all the aircraft flown by the 199th FIG since its inception in 1946, the F-86Ls were perhaps the most strikingly marked, this preserved specimen wearing full 1961 unit colours

**Left** The Sabre era finally came to an end in January 1961 when the first of the mighty Convair F-102A Delta Daggers arrived at Hickam. Over the next four months the 199th received more 'Dueces' from frontline units in Okinawa and the Philippines. Armed with Hughes AIM-4 Falcon air-to-air guided missiles, and fitted with an MG-10 radar fire control system, the F-102 provided a quantum leap forward for the 'Guard, the aircraft's top speed of 825 mph allowed the HANGmen to signal their presence over the islands with endless sonic booms. As with the P-47N, the 199th continued to fly the F-102 long after all other 'Guard units had received F-4s or F-106s, the unit eventually retiring their 'Deuces' in 1976. Immaculately preserved, this F-102 is rather surprisingly marked up in South-East Asian Colours rather than the far more familiar Air Defense Command (ADC) grey

**Above** Continuing the SEA theme at Hickam is the last remaining F-4C on base, 63-7540 looking rather odd in its browns and greens, particularly with the TAC-style base code sprayed on the fin. Like its former squadron mates, this aircraft was named after a Hawaiian bird late in its service life, '7540 being christened 'Mamo'. Although this aircraft looks resplendent in its camouflage, one hopes that the next time the airframe is resprayed, the veteran F-4 will emerge wearing 'Egypt One' grey overall, and a full colour lei on the fin

Something of a mystery machine, this preserved Cessna 0-2A sits quietly alongside the P-40K at Wheeler Field. Officially, none of these robust little Cessnas were based in the islands, although one suspects that this airframe may have been 'acquired' by the 199th to act as a forward air controlling (FAC) spotter aircraft for operations out over the ranges when the unit had F-4Cs. Officially assigned to seven ANG units, the 0-2s fulfilled the FAC role throughout the 1970s, these aircraft eventually being replaced by Cessna OA-37Bs in the early 1980s